Reptile Keeper's Guides

RED-TAILED BOAS AND RELATIVES

R. D. Bartlett
Patricia Bartlett

BARRON'S

Acknowledgments

For sharing information and opinions, and for allowing us
the opportunity to photograph boas, we thank Rob MacInnes
and Chuck Hurt of Glades Herp, Inc.; Carl May; Bob
Guerriere of Bob Guerriere's Ancient Reproductions; Eugene
Bessette of Ophiological Services; Gus Rentfro of Rio Bravo
Reptiles; Regis Opferman; Rich Ihle and John Bergman of
salmonboa.com; and Chris McQuade and Sheila Rodgers
of Gulf Coast Reptiles.

A special note of thanks to Paul Hollander for explaining
Genetics 101 to us, to our reviewer, David M. Schleser of
Nature's Images, for his pertinent comments, and to our
editor, Pat Hunter, for helping us smooth some of the
rougher written terrain.

All inquiries should be addressed to:
Barron's Educational Series, Inc.
250 Wireless Boulevard
Hauppauge, NY 11788
http://www.barronseduc.com

Library of Congress Catalog Card No. 2002033232

International Standard Book No. 0-7641-2279-7

Library of Congress Cataloging-in-Publication Data
Bartlett, Richard D., 1938–
    Red-tailed boas and relatives / R. D. Bartlett, Patricia Bartlett.
        p.   cm. — (Reptile keeper's guides)
    ISBN 0-7641-2279-7
        1. Boa constrictors as pets. I. Title.

SF459.S5 B375   2003
639.3′967—dc21   2002033232

Printed in Hong Kong
9 8 7 6 5 4 3 2 1

Contents

Preface

My first boa was purchased in the early 1950s, while I was in junior high school. I acquired a copy of a magazine called *Outdoor Life,* and thumbed through the magazine until I came to the ads in the back. A company called Quivira Specialties Company offered "common boas" for about $3 each. The even more exotic-sounding "red-tailed boas" were more expensive, about $5. (The owners of Quivira, herpetologists Charles E. and Mae D. Burt, of Topeka, Kansas, were minor folk heroes in the small world of herp hobbyists at the time.) Each and every snake Quivira offered was a wild-collected import, straight from the jungle; captive breeding of any kind of snake was still a decade or so away.

In those pre–credit card days, impulse purchases were impossible.

It took me weeks of scrimping to acquire the money necessary for a boa, then additional days of weighing what I supposed was the heightened beauty of the red-tail against the more affordable cost of the common boa. Finally a decision was made and I hiked to the post office to buy and send a money order. Then I hiked back home, to agonize for the next couple of weeks about my rash decision—for the red-tail had won! I had "gambled" an extra $2 on what was still then an unknown element. As it turned out, it was a prudent purchase. The snake that arrived was magnificent, healthy, and worth every penny of the purchase price.

Although the importation of boas is now more regulated (the members of the family Boidae are regulated by CITES—Convention on International Trade in Endangered Species), these snakes remain readily available. Wild-caught examples may be difficult or impossible to acquire due to low exportation quotas or export prohibitions. The good news is that the numbers of boas now being bred in captivity can largely meet the demand, even for unusual color, pattern, or geographic morphs.

Dick and Patti Bartlett

A pretty baby Peruvian boa lies atop a forest leaf.

What Is a Red-tailed Boa?

What is a red-tailed boa? Is it really different from a common boa?

Actually, the red-tail and the common boa are just two of some nine subspecies of the boa constrictor.

Generally speaking, boa constrictors are neotropical constricting snakes that feed upon warm-blooded prey, with small mammals and birds being the primary fare. Younger or smaller boas feed upon small mammals, or rarely upon lizards or tree frogs.

All boa constrictor subspecies are differentiated by color, pattern, and area of origin. (The area of origin also determines to some extent the size of the animal found there.) For instance, the red-tail, *Boa constrictor constrictor*, has a brighter red (often maroon) coloration on the tail than its well-known conspecific, the common boa, *Boa constrictor imperator*.

The boa constrictors are found from northwestern Mexico through South America and on some of the surrounding islands. The red-tailed boa occupies a portion of this range, being found in rain forest habitat across much of northern and central South America, including the Amazon Basin.

Lighter than most boas from Amazonian Peru, this baby was found near the port city of Iquitos.

The red-tails with the prefix of Guyanan, Suriname, Peruvian, and Brazilian, are red-tails, of course, but are from different geographic areas within the red-tail range. There may be slight differences in color, but so far no taxonomist has thought these to be constant or substantial enough to erect additional subspecies. You're dependent on your retailer or breeder for information on the geographic origin of your snake.

Today, other descriptive terms have been added, terms such as hypomelanistic, salmon, coral-bellied, Hog Island, albino, snow, and Arabesque. These describe either the origin or the coloration of the boas available in the pet market of 2003. Some of these "newer" forms occur naturally, and are now being seen only

Comparative Prices of Baby Boa Constrictor Subspecies and Color Variants in 2003

- Bolivian (also called Brazilian silver-backs), *Boa constrictor amarali*, $200–$400
- Red-tailed, *Boa constrictor constrictor*
    - Colombian, $85–$125
    - Guyanan, $175–$300
    - Peruvian, $225–$350
    - Suriname, $250–$300
    - (Brazilians are not currently available.)
- Common, *Boa constrictor imperator*
    - Mexican, $75–$150
    - Central American, $65–$100
    - Colombian, $65–$100
    - Hog Island, $250
- Long-tailed, *Boa constrictor longicauda*, $250–$400
- Clouded, *Boa constrictor nebulosa*, seldom available in the United States, $1,500
- St. Lucia boa, *Boa constrictor orophias*, not commercially available in the United States
- Argentine, *Boa constrictor occidentalis*, $100–$300. Cost varies by color, with those having the most pink in the dorsal coloration being the most expensive.
- Albino boas (various subspecies and genetic strains), $800–$3,500
- Ghost boas (various subspecies), $3,000–$4,000
- Snow boas (various lineages), $3,500–$5,500
- Salmon boas, $400–$1,000
- Anerythristic, $200–$400

because boas are currently being imported from areas of tropical America only recently accessible to us. Other colors (and patterns) now being seen in herpetoculture are the result of genetic chance or deliberate selective breeding by hobbyists.

But let's start with the basics about red-tails, common, and other boa constrictors.

Other than the intensity of the tail color, there is a slight difference in head pattern between the red-tail and the common boa. Both have a spear point down the center of the head; the red-tail has lateral projections off the spear point at the level of the eyes. There is also a very real difference in the cost factor. A baby common boa may be priced at $75 to $125, while

A portrait of a Costa Rican boa.

a baby red-tail will go for essentially twice that, $175 to $250.

Are the snakes worth the difference in cost? That will depend entirely on you. Do you prefer to have a snake with a red to maroon tail or one with a brownish red tail? Both are equally hardy, both attain about the same length, and both eat the same food. So, if you want a red-tail, you will be paying a premium price for color alone.

Is color worth the price difference? It is if you feel it is. Each boa, like any other reptile, is worth whatever the seller, and you, the buyer, agree it is worth.

The long-tailed boa (photographed at Glades Herp) hails from northwestern Peru.

This 6-foot-long (183-cm) Peruvian boa was photographed in the rain forest on Peru's Rio Orosa.

The Red-tailed Boa at a Glance

Common name: Red-tailed boa constrictor
Scientific name: *Boa constrictor constrictor*
Other boa constrictor subspecies: Nine, of which two (*B. c. nebulosa* and *B. c. orophias*) are occasionally considered full species. There are several well-defined boa constrictor color variations, most of island (insular) distribution.

Habitat and size: This beautiful and powerful snake is a neotropical, rain forest representative of the snake family Boidae (the boas and pythons). Although not as large as other members of the family, the red-tailed boa, with an adult size of 10 to 12 feet (301–366 cm), is still considered to be one of the world's giant snakes. In the neotropics, the red-tailed boa is exceeded in size only by some species of anacondas (water boas).

Prey: Captive red-tailed boas prefer mammalian prey (captives are usually provided prekilled rodents). Live prey is killed by constriction, which essentially equates to suffocation. If your red-tail is not accustomed to prekilled prey, we suggest that you acclimate it to prekilled prey as quickly as possible (see chapter on feeding, pages 28–30).

Reproduction: The red-tailed boa produces its young alive. A clutch can consist of as few as two to more than seventy babies. Neonates usually measure between 14 and 18 inches (35–46 cm) in length. Gestation may vary from 5.5 to 6.5 months; those boas from cooler areas have longer gestation than those from warmer climes. A healthy female may breed annually, but a successful breeding every second year is not uncommon. Birth of the babies is often correlated with a drop in barometric pressure (such as during the passages of a weather-front system).

Disposition: Although they may be a little snappy when first received, red-tailed boas usually tame readily and rapidly. After only a few gentle handlings, these snakes seldom show any

Despite their brilliant color, boas, such as this Brazilian specimen, blend remarkably well with a leafy background.

Hog Island boas have a pale and changeable coloration and may be of small size.

A portrait of a long-tailed boa.

Note the vertically elliptical pupils on this Peruvian boa.

evidence of a bad temper. However, as the snakes acclimate to captive conditions, they tend to associate the opening of the cage with food, and their feeding response can be very rapid. Do not attempt to handle your boa without washing your hands after touching mice, rats, or other prey items.

Red-tailed boas are generally rather slow moving, slow to take fright, and prone to holding securely to you when they are being lifted or moved. Adult male boas are territorial and may actively fight with other males. Their teeth can produce slashing wounds. Combating males will often also attempt to bite an interceding human. Use extreme care, especially in dealing with a boa 5 feet (152 cm) or more in length.

Additional comments: Although red-tailed boas may be active during the hours of daylight, they prowl most persistently at dusk and for a few hours after darkness has fallen. Should a boa prove reluctant to eat, try feeding it in the evening.

The Boa as a Pet

Boa Identification

In general, boa constrictors are heavy-bodied but supple snakes that kill their prey by constriction. They have myriad small, nonkeeled scales. Varying by subspecies, the anterior body is tan, light brown, dark brown, or gray, with dark dorsal saddles that may or may not have forward and rearward dorso-lateral extensions. A series of lighter vertically elongated spots or ocelli occur along each side. There is a dark marking between the eyes and another on each side of the face. Near the tail, the tan of the body usually becomes paler and the dark dorsal blotches become even darker (brownish red, orange, maroon, or almost black) and

This Costa Rican boa is lighter in color than many examples.

are usually outlined in black. Generally speaking, those from the rain forest are more brightly colored/patterned than those from islands.

Neonates are usually noticeably paler than the adults.

Both the young and the adults have eyes that are quite similar to the body in coloration and have vertically elliptical pupils. The labial scales are well defined but lack true heat-sensing pits. (Neither the subcaudals—scales on the underside of the tail—nor the anal plate is divided.)

Boas have a pair of cloacal spurs—remaining vestiges of bygone days when snakes had legs. The spurs of the males are larger than those of the females.

The red-tail and the common boa are only two of the several subspecies of this big snake. Two others now kept and bred by hobbyists are the some-what bland-colored Bolivian boa, *B. c. amarali,* and the dark (but often quite attractive) Argentine boa, *B. c. occiden-talis.* Some less well-known subspecies are the northwestern Peruvian boa, *B. c. ortonii,* the black-bellied boa, *B. c. melanogaster,* and the long-tailed boa, *B. c. longicauda,* all of western South America. Insular forms include the Tres Marias boa, *B. c. sigma,* the St. Lucia boa, *B. c. orophias,* and the clouded boa, *B. c. nebulosa.*

Because the snakes themselves are variable, the criteria differentiating the various subspecies of boa constrictors vary. In some cases, it is the number of ventral scutes (the large belly scales) and the number of scale rows (excluding the belly scales) at midbody. Trying to count these on a live, determined-to-escape boa can be a real challenge.

The Common Boa

Because of their immense north-to-south range (northern Mexico to the scrublands and coastal [non-rain forest] areas of tropical Colombia and Venezuela, and an introduced population in Miami) you may see common boas, *Boa constrictor imperator,*

An adult Colombian boa.

marketed as Mexican or Colombian boas. Those from a few of the Central American islands may be referred to as Corn Island or Hog Island boas. Common boas also exhibit a great variation in color. Many from the north are quite dark, those from coastal islands laved by the balmy Caribbean are prone to pinkish or orangish hues, and Panamanian and Colombian examples are creamy tan and brown (sometimes with pale orange overtones). Most of the common boas seen in the American pet trade come from Colombia.

The variable common boa has fewer than 253 ventral scales and

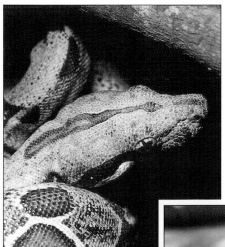

A neonate Colombian boa.

The dwarfed boas from Corn Island are of dark color and have a reddish hue.

9

between 55 and 79 rows of dorsal scales at midbody. The dorsal blotches from anterior nape to above the vent number 22 or more. As currently understood, the boas once designated as *B. c. eques* (Payta, Peru), *B. c. isthmica* (Darien region of Panama), *B. c. mexicana* (Mexico and northern Central America), and *B. c. sabogae* (Saboga and Taboga Islands, Panama) are invalid synonyms of *B. c. imperator*.

Hog Island Boa

Although in the wild the Hog Island boa (from Cayos Cocinos, Honduras) is a fairly small morph (4 to 6 feet [122–183 cm] long) of the common boa, captives may grow considerably larger. Adult size seems predicated on the frequency with which the snakes eat and on the food value of the prey. Insular boas feed on what they can find, which tends to be ectothermic creatures such as frogs, lizards, perhaps crabs. When fed the typically rich diet of lab rodents (rich when compared to island resources, at least), the Hog Island boa can grow to more than 8 feet (244 cm).

The color-changing ability of the Hog Island boa quickly caught the interest of hobbyists as much as its small size. The head and anterior body of the Hog Island boa are of very light tan or cream coloration; the flanks and tail saddles may be pink or orange. Brilliant pinks and oranges are usually much more in evidence at night. It is paler and less contrastingly patterned by day.

Island Boas

From the Corn Islands of Nicaragua come orange common boas with well-defined patterns; from Taboguilla, Saboga, and Taboga Islands, Panama, come orange common boas with indistinct dorsal markings; and from Crawl Key, Belize (and surrounding islands) come pale gray to pinkish gray boas bearing a variable amount of black flecking.

Northwest Peruvian Boa

The Northwest Peruvian boa, *B. c. ortonii*, is an arid land boa of variable appearance and questionable taxonomic validity. It is of rather pale coloration and has a hazy, often poorly defined dorsal pattern. It is probably synonymous with *B. c. constrictor*. Despite its nomenclatural uncertainty, hobbyists continue to use the designation of *B. c. ortonii*, and when it is available, it is one of the more costly of the boas.

Red-tails

The red-tailed boa is nearly as variable in coloration as the common boa. Whether red-tails hail from southern Colombia, Guyana, Suriname, Peru, or Amazonian Brazil, they are pale when

Neonates of Hog Island boas usually lack strongly contrasting colors.

babies, but the colors often intensify with adulthood. Typically, the color of the tail may intensify to red-orange (southern Colombia and Venezuela) or a blood red or deep maroon (Amazon Basin and southeast of the Basin, respectively), but there is much overlap in color. This subspecies is somewhat less busily patterned than the common boa, having fewer than 20 dorsal saddles. The ventral scales number 250 or fewer and 81 to 95 scale rows encircle the snake at mid-body. Like the common boa, the red-tail, the Amazon Basin representative of the group, has an immense range. It is eagerly sought by hobbyists.

Juveniles of the long-tailed boa are very strongly patterned.

Silver-backed, Brazilian, or Bolivian Boa

The boa from southern Brazil, eastern Bolivia, and adjacent Paraguay is often referred to as the silver-backed, the Brazilian, or the Bolivian boa. It is specifically designated *B. c. amarali*. Although it is a coveted subspecies, it is not as richly colored as its Amazonian counterparts, instead having a grayish ground color that may be heavily speckled with black, and a deep purplish maroon or blackish red tail. Although like all other boas, this race is variable in certain key characteristics, having fewer than 237 ventral scutes, between 55 and 79 dorsal scale rows, and extensions on the dark dorsal markings that connect them into a chainlike arrangement; it is usually identifiable to subspecies.

Argentine Boa

Dark (but variable) in coloration at all stages of its life, the Argentine boa has been all but overlooked by hobbyists

until fairly recently. Today (2003), however, captive breeding programs are perpetuating some of the prettiest Argentines, and prices, once exorbitantly high, have moderated. No longer routinely exported from Paraguay and Argentina, the presence of this snake in the pet trade is now very dependent on successful breeding

The Bolivian boa.

Madagascar Boas

The island continent of Madagascar, east of Africa across the Mozambique Channel, is home to three boas that were long ascribed to two genera—*Acrantophis* and *Sanzinia*—but equally long recognized as being closely related to the red-tailed boa. In 1991 it was determined by taxonomic researcher Arnold Kluge that the three Madagascar species were actually members of the genus *Boa*. To date, this nomenclature has not been generally accepted, but it may eventually be. Should this occur, the two ground boas would become *Boa dumerilii* (Dumeril's boa) and *Boa madagascariensis* (Madagascar ground boa), rather than be part of the genus *Acrantophis*.

The Madagascar tree boa presents a different nomenclatural problem. Since its specific name of *madagascariensis* is identical to that of the ground boa, which has precedence, if the tree boa is treated as a member of the genus *Boa*, its specific name will be changed to *mandrita*. Occasionally, and in error, you may see reference made to *Sanzinia mandrita* when, if *Sanzinia* is used as the genus, the species name should be *madagascariensis*.

These three snakes are varying shades of quiet browns, tans, olives, and creams. The two species of ground boas undergo very little ontogenetic change, the neonates looking like somewhat paler miniatures of the adults. However, the tree boa usually undergoes a considerable change of color. Tree boa neonates usually have a ground color of brown, orange, or red. With age and growth this dulls to olive or olive-brown. About 40 light-edged darker bars (often triangles) are present along the length of this snake.

Dumeril's boa (top) and Madagascan ground boa (bottom), both of Madagascar, are becoming increasingly common in the American pet trade.

programs. This boa has 22 to 30 dorsal saddles, fewer than 88 rows of scales at midbody, and about 250 ventral scales.

Black-bellied Boa
In 1983 a dark-colored "red-tailed" boa from the forested areas of Ecuador was described. The common name of black-bellied boa was assigned. The subspecific name of *melanogaster* alludes to the dark venter of the population. This boa is seldom seen in captivity. Although the nomenclature is accepted as valid by some authorities, it is questioned by others.

Long-tailed or Black-tailed Boa
Boa constrictor longicauda is known as the long-tailed boa or the black-tailed boa. It has more recently been referred to as the "Peruvian black-tailed boa" by dealers. A rather recently described Peruvian form, the tail of this race is only marginally (if any) longer than that of its conspecifics. Given the natural variances so commonly seen throughout boa populations, the question of tail length and corresponding subcaudal scale count seems rather indefinite criteria for determining subspecific status. However, the neonates are very cleanly and precisely marked, and do look quite different from the surrounding races.

Clouded Boa
From the Lesser Antillian islands of Dominica and St. Lucia come two busily patterned boa subspecies. The first of these is the Clouded boa, *B. c. nebulosa*, of Dominica. As indicated by both its common and scientific names, the markings of this boa race are obscured (clouded) with dark

Bob Guerriere specializes in breeding super-pink Argentine boas.

pigment. While not particularly pretty, it is different enough to be in demand by hobbyists. Other than island of origin, the identifying characteristics of the clouded boa are a ventral scute count of from 258 to 273 and 32 to 35 dorsal blotches.

St. Lucia Boa
The very similar St. Lucia boa, *B. c. orophias*, hails from further south in the Lesser Antilles. It is restricted to the island of St. Lucia. It, too, is a dusky race, but the saddles are well in evidence. The tail markings of this

Clouded boas are seldom available to hobbyists.

The Argentine Boa—
The New Snake on the Block

This southernmost representative of the genus is a red-tailed boa with virtually no red. Despite this, the Argentine boa is fast gaining in popularity among American herpetoculturists. Although some lineages of this snake are prettily marked with pale pink, peach, or light orange on the otherwise dark dorsal saddles, not even these could be called brightly colored. Most specimens are merely dark-on-dark snakes with an opalescent overlay and some brownish tan at the perimeters of the dorsal saddles and lateral markings. While the colors dull with age, the opalescence remains.

Disposition

Not so long ago Argentine boas were difficult to sell. Coupled with the dark coloration, these boas had (and still do have) the reputation for having an attitude problem. Hobbyists simply didn't seem interested in the big, dark snakes with the big, dark dispositions.

This no longer seems to be the case. Not only are Argentine boas selling briskly in their own right, but herpetoculturists striving for new and paler albino boas are working the big, dark snakes into breeding programs with other races. Because of the prevalence of dark pigment (melanin) when bred into an albino program, the resulting offspring are much whiter than normal. Argentine boas, bad disposition and all, are in demand.

Actually, the attitude of the Argentine boa is not much different from that of many Mexican boas and of some red-tailed boas. When babies, or if wild-collected, the snakes huff, puff, feint with open mouth, and, if you're intimidated enough to be hesitant about grasping them, they will bite. However, if you overlook the bluff and quickly and gently grasp and lift the snakes, they usually abruptly end the blustery overture and allow themselves to be handled with impunity. Even if they do bite, the aggression is more disconcerting than painful. If handled regularly, the snakes quickly outgrow the tendency to bite.

Temperature Preferences

As would be expected from a snake hailing from well south of the equator, the Argentine boa is far more tolerant of cool temperatures than the more tropical red-tails. It also seems to take cooler winter temperatures to cycle them for breeding. Nighttime temperatures during the winter cooling period may be as low as 60°F (15.5°C), with daytime temperatures rising into the low 80s (27°C).

An Argentine boa from the Guerriere line.

A pink-saddled Argentine boa baby of the Eugene Bessette strain.

Breeding

Both in the wild and in captivity, Argentine boas breed most readily, and successfully, during the shortest days of the year. They may begin their breeding sequence in the autumn, just as the temperatures begin to cool, during the winter cooling period, or as the temperatures begin to warm in the spring. More successful breedings seem to occur in the spring than at other times. As with other races of boas, copulation can last for several hours. Although in the wild, where conditions are harsher than in captivity, breeding may occur only biennially, amply fed captive female Argentine boas successfully breed annually. Females give birth in the mid- to late summer.

Methods to succeed with these boas vary, but some of the more successful breeders provide daytime temperatures of 105 to 110°F (40–43°C) for gestating females. Nighttime temperatures are 10 to 15°F cooler. Although females do occasionally spend considerable time at the cool end of the cage, they seem to revel in the heat, and may bask for long periods.

Females of this race of boa become sexually mature when as small as 6 feet (183 cm). Large adults attain a length of 9 feet (270 cm). The largest females produce the largest clutches (neonates from these have numbered in the mid-50s).

Feeding

Neonates are eager feeders and sufficiently large to consume fair-size mice or small rat pups. With growth the size of the prey should be routinely increased. An adult Argentine boa can easily swallow and digest 4- to 5-pound (1.8–2.3 kg) rabbits. The larger the meal, the more important it is that cage temperatures are not only warm enough for digestion, but rather stable as well. As with other boas, improper cage temperatures will cause the snakes to regurgitate.

Neonate boas, such as this Argentine one belonging to Eugene Bessette, are barely a handful.

subspecies are nearly black with cream-colored crossmarks. The tail of the clouded boa is usually somewhere on the reddish side of black.

Although island of origin remains the best identifying feature, *B. c. orophias* has between 270 and 288 ventral scutes and from 27 to 31 dorsal blotches.

Tres Marias Boa

Reference is sometimes made to a third (questionable) island race, the Tres Marias boa, *B. c. sigma* (Tres Marias Islands, Pacific Mexico). It is most similar in appearance to *B. c. imperator*, from which it differs in having a higher ventral scute count (270–288 against fewer than 253). It has 30 or fewer dorsal blotches.

Handling Your Boa

Of the various boa subspecies, several forms, including the northern examples of the common boa (often referred to as the Mexican boa) and the Argentine boa, have a reputation for defensive or aggressive biting. In reality, a bad disposition, or, conversely, a good one, can occur in any of the subspecies or color phases.

A manifestation of either good or bad disposition is an individual trait. As juveniles many boas bite defensively, some upon the slightest provocation, only to become entirely tractable when larger. Frequent, gentle handling will often do much to quiet down a "biter." Wild-collected boas, especially those of larger sizes, are often more apt to bite than captive-bred boas—and remember, the bigger the boa, the bigger its mouth, and those teeth *hurt!* Boas with vision impaired by an impending shed are also prone to bite.

There are just a few basic guidelines for handling your boa.

• Always remember that a snake—especially a nervous snake—handled soon after eating may regurgitate its meal. (If a monster 200 times your own weight lifted and dangled you around after you'd eaten a steak dinner, you might regurgitate, too.) Do not lift your boa for a few days after it has eaten.

• Boas typically respond defensively to fast movements, but are more tolerant of slow ones.

• Snakes typically shy away from movements above them, but are somewhat less wary of movements from the side. Thus, approaching your boa slowly from the side is less apt to result in a defensive strike by the animal than swooping down from above. Many boas react adversely to having their head approached or touched. Until the boa is accustomed to being handled, some hobbyists prefer to first lift the snake with a snake hook and then transfer it to their hands. This will allow handling while minimizing the potential for being bitten.

• Do not grasp your snake by its neck. Rather, slide one hand under it about a third of the way back from the head, the other hand about a quarter of the way forward from the tail tip, and, holding the snake loosely, lift it slowly. If not startled or frightened, the snake will probably establish contact with you. Keep it away from your face. If sufficiently frightened, a restrained boa may void the contents of its cloaca on its captor. Wash your hands thoroughly if this happens to you, although the odor alone will probably make this admonition unnecessary.

Biting

Remember, even if it does bite and constrict, a bite by a baby boa may startle you, can even hurt you, and often draws blood, but it is not dangerous. Pulling sharply away if bitten, even though that is a typical response, may cause the boa's teeth to break off in the wound. Instead, though it may be difficult for you to do, if the snake doesn't release immediately, bend down, place the snake on a flat surface, and release your grip on its body. It will almost invariably release its hold within moments. Even as a baby, the snake knows you are too big to eat. It is entirely possible that you smell and taste unnatural, as well. (Please don't take this personally!)

The bite by a boa larger than 3 feet (91 cm) can be far more serious, and it may take a second person to help you disengage the constricting coils. (Do not try to handle a boa longer than 8 feet [244 cm] without someone else nearby; the snake's strength can be dangerous.) If you do get bitten,

cleanse the bite site carefully and allow the snake to settle down before you try to handle it again. Persistence on your part will usually result in your having an easily handled boa.

Important Considerations

Now let's proceed onward to the keeping of the red-tailed boa and its relatives.

Once acclimated, these are usually easily kept snakes. Of all the boa constrictors, we consider babies of both common and Argentine boas the best beginners' snakes. Both of these snakes are a little more tolerant of temperature fluctuations and seem less apt to regurgitate meals when disturbed. The imported red-tailed boas and Bolivian boas are somewhat more prone to regurgitation, so we urge that only feeding, captive-bred babies be purchased, and suggest that even these may be best suited for somewhat advanced hobbyists.

But, with this all now said, we urge that you carefully consider your purchase *before the fact*. The keeping of a

Mexican boas can be quite dark—both in color and disposition.

This is a very pretty, large Colombian boa.

Boas climb readily and well, as shown by this Bolivian boa.

boa is a long-term project. With good care, these snakes will live for more than 15 years, and some have lived for more than 40 years. And these snakes grow—within the first two years, the very easily handled and kept 14- to 16-inch-long (35–40 cm) baby can attain a length of 6 feet (183 cm). Within another year or two the same snake may measure more than 8 feet (244 cm) long and could reach 12 feet (366 cm) when it is fully adult. While baby boas sell readily, it is usually a very real problem to find a new home for an adult. Besides having to face both handling and caging problems, the specter of liability is very real. Nature centers, zoos, and museums already have all the boas they need. Some municipalities now prohibit the keeping of snakes more than 6 feet

(183 cm) in length, and it seems that other cities/towns consider a snake over 6 feet too large to be considered a pet.

How to Find and Where to Buy Your Red-tailed Boa

Although boas of some type have always been available in the pet trade, today the variety of boas is greater than ever.

Of all the boa varieties, the common boas from Colombia are the least expensive subspecies and are usually seen in pet stores. Since most females on the boa farms in Colombia give birth at about the same time, large numbers of babies become available in the pet trade simultaneously. It is then, of course, that prices are the lowest.

Obtaining Your Boas

Because many of the subspecies and color morphs of the boa constrictor are quite (to exorbitantly) expensive, you won't find them in neighborhood pet shops. Instead, you may have to search out the snake from a specialty dealer or a breeder listed in the classified ads in a reptile magazine or via the World Wide Web. Once you've located the snake, you might be able to pick it up directly from the dealer. In other cases—in fact, in most cases—it will be necessary to have the snake shipped to you.

From wherever they may be, hobbyist-breeders or specialist-dealers will be able to ship the boa you want to you. The advent of the Internet and digital cameras has brought to both purchaser and dealer another benefit: In most cases you will be able to view a picture of the actual boa in which you are interested. While this may not be as good as actually seeing the boa before you buy it, it is a gigantic step upward from the days of blind sales.

Reptile swap meets or "expos" are excellent sources of specimens. These get-togethers of breeders and potential purchasers are now held in many of the larger cities across the United States and Europe. These expos may vary in size from only a dozen or so vendors to some that host more than 400 vendors. One of the largest of these, an event held annually in central Florida, has 500 vendor tables and more than 10,000 attendees.

But whether your purchase is from the Web or at an expo, we caution you to know both the product you seek and the vendor who sells it.

Shipping: When purchasing a snake on the Web, the chances are excellent that it will be shipped to you by air. Although airport-to-airport air freight remains the preference of many shippers, several alternate freight companies offer a very convenient door-to-door service. Whichever you choose, in most cases you will pay for both the animal and the shipping charges in advance. Your shipper will need your credit card number and expiration date, a money order, or a cashier's check. Many shippers will accept personal checks but wait until the check clears the bank before shipping (usually within a week or so).

Another payment method is COD, but this is both more expensive and more inconvenient than the pre-paid method.

Most shipments take about 24 hours to get from the shipper to the purchaser. Shipping may become difficult, and should be avoided, during very hot weather, very cold weather, or during the peak holiday travel/shipping/mailing times.

Once your shipment has arrived, claim it as quickly as possible. This is especially important in bad (either too hot or too cold) weather. Learn the hours of your cargo office and whether the shipment can be picked up at the ticket counter if it arrives after the cargo office has closed.

After paying the applicable charges, open and inspect your shipment before leaving the cargo facility. Unless otherwise specified, reliable shippers guarantee live delivery. However, if there is a problem, both the shipper and the airline(s) will require a "carrier's discrepancy" or "damage" report made out, signed and dated by carrier personnel. In the very rare case when a problem has occurred, insist on the filling out and filing of a claim form right then and contact your shipper immediately for instructions.

Although this may initially sound complicated, you will probably find that the transportation by air of the boa you want is easy, fast, and safe. However, it is not always inexpensive. Be sure to check the relative charges assessed by all carriers.

Kinds and Colors

Within the last few years, the production of designer colors of genus *Boa* has skyrocketed. Some interesting colors and patterns have proven not to be genetically heritable. Others are, and their lineage has been stabilized, and in some cases additionally embellished. If you're familiar with the color morphs of other snake species, particularly the larger pythons and boas, you'll recognize some of the descriptions and terms used here.

Striped Boas

Partial or full striping was one of the first mutations to catch the eye of hobbyists. First seen on imported common and red-tailed boas, the pattern did not prove genetically replicable. It was eventually determined that most of the cases of striping resulted from somewhat suboptimal gestation temperatures. Today, through working with those examples that were not caused by temperature manipulation, striped boas have been developed, and in at least some cases, the pretty pattern has been genetically stabilized. Seldom entire, the striping is more often restricted to either the tail of the snake or its body.

Arabesque: In 1989, in a clutch of otherwise normal-appearing common boa babies, another unique color and pattern occurred. Besides having dark speckling on the head, sides, and to a lesser degree along the back, the boas had a reduced number of dark crossbars, and heavy, dark, dorsolateral striping. Best yet, the pattern has proven to be genetically replicable. This interesting morph is now called the Arabesque boa.

Albinos

The arrival of imported albino boas has always caused more than just a stir of interest among herpetoculturists. In reptiles, albinism has a different effect than in mammals. It is merely the lack of black pigment (or amelanism), a condition that allows the yellow and red pigments and the reflections from the iridiophores to take on a new intensity. All colors *except* black will be represented.

To make things even more interesting, albinism in reptiles—boas included—takes several forms, meaning that more than one gene locus is involved. As a result, it is entirely possible to breed together two albino boas and have all normal-appearing babies in the resulting clutch. The neonates will, however, be heterozygous for both strains of albinism.

Striping can be caused by adverse gestating temperatures or genetics. This beautiful boa originated in Suriname.

An overview of the Arabesque boa.

Albinism has been incorporated into striped and motley boas, as well as the normal phase.

Hypomelanistic Boas

The term hypomelanistic refers to boas lacking most black pigment but that are not albinos. Both the salmon and super salmon boas fall under this heading, but there seem to be several strains and intensities of salmon. Even more brightly colored are the hypos now being called blood boas. The parent stock of these originated from El Salvador.

Sunglow-albino: Sunglow boas have resulted from breeding an albino boa with a hypomelanistic boa. The ground color varies, but is usually of some shade of orange or yellow-orange and the tail coloration is coral. This is a startlingly beautiful, and very high-priced, color morph.

Motley: Motley boas have the light dorsal blotches reduced to a series of well separated rounded spots. The dark crossbands are greatly widened and largely contiguous.

Anerythristic Boas

Anerythristic boas lack red pigment, hence are often black and white(ish) in color. Although in itself not one of the prettier color phases, crosses between anerythristic boas *and* albino boas have allowed the development of the snow boa.

Ghost: Ghost boas were derived by crossing hypomelanistic boas with anerythristic boas. Ghost boas have a silvery or frosty overlay to their scales.

Paradox: The paradox pattern was another spontaneously appearing morph that manifested itself only a few years ago. Both of the parents of the first paradox boas were heterozygous for albinism. The male was an intergrade common x red-tailed boa, and the female was a pure common boa of Colombian lineage. The paradox in this equation was the appearance of small, scattered patches of black pigment on neonates that were otherwise obvious

Sunglow boas were developed by Rich Ihle of salmonboa.com. A normally colored male is pictured at left; a beautiful rose sunglow morph, below. Photos by John Bergman.

albinos. It is not yet known whether this is a genetically replicable trait.

Snow: Snow boas are much whiter than albinos. Clad in scales of white and yellow, typically the areas normally dark in a wild boa are no more than a dusky suffusion. Their lineage includes both albino and anerythristic parents.

Assuredly, as breeding programs mature, new, exciting colors and patterns of boa constrictors will be developed and offered.

Understanding Selective Breeding

Selective breeding (linebreeding) of a boa is not necessarily always in pursuit of albinism, unusual pattern, or other aberrant characteristic. Rather, it can be a sustained effort to merely assure that certain desired traits remain stabilized. The red-tailed boa is one example. The intense coloration and definitive markings of this have long made it popular.

Linebreeding involves breeding together the paired boas having the most desirable characteristics, then breeding and rebreeding parent with offspring, or the pair with the most desirable patterns, upgrading and diversifying the gene pool whenever possible. It may take generations of effort to develop and stabilize a given trait, or you may be lucky and have a significant breakthrough occur in only a generation or two.

The progeny of any given union may look like either or both of the parents, but may occasionally be of very different appearance.

As you selectively breed your boas you should be aware of four primary terms: allele, heterozygous, homozygous, and tyrosinase. Defined, an allele is a gene, homozygous means having two identical alleles for a given trait, heterozygous means having non-identical alleles for that given trait, and tyrosinase is a copper-containing enzyme that figures prominently in melanin production.

In everyday parlance, homozygous herps breed true for a given trait. In heterozygous specimens, the recessive trait is present but masked. Boas that are heterozygous for a trait may look normal, but their offspring may look different.

If a gene is recessive, then both parents must contribute a recessive gene for that gene's characteristic to appear. Two purple-spotted parents could have a red-striped baby. A dominant trait is the gene that gives the animal or plant its appearance; if a gene is dominant for purple spots, all the offspring will have purple spots.

When you breed two normal or two albino boas together (we'll ignore the tyrosinase factor for this example), the resulting offspring are usually similar in appearance to the parents. That's fairly straightforward.

But then you start out with an adult normally colored female and an adult albino male. The snakes breed and you hope "Wow—albino babies!" The babies are born and all of them are the normal color of the female. What has happened? (Check Punnett Square, Figure 1.)

	A	A
a	aA	aA
a	aA	aA

Figure 1.

This is a clutch of common boas, some still in the amniotic membrane. Photo by Gopher Carlson.

In reality, everything is absolutely normal—exactly the way it should be. The babies that have just been born, called the F1 generation, look normally colored, but they are each heterozygous for albinism; they have one gene for albinism, and one for normal coloration. The normal coloration gene (A) masks or is dominant over the albino gene (a). If you breed one of the female babies back with the albino male, statistically the clutch should (and probably will) contain 50 percent albinos and 50 percent normally colored hatchlings (see Punnett Square, Figure 2). There are two phenotypes resulting from this breeding: the aa and the aA.

	a	A
a	aa	aA
a	aa	aA

Figure 2.

But what happens if you breed a heterozygous baby to a heterozygous sibling of the opposite sex?

Statistically, the clutch from such a union will contain 25 percent albinos, 25 percent normals, and 50 percent heterozygous babies that are of normal coloration. That's three phenotypes. *Except through breeding trials, it is impossible for a hobbyist to ascertain which of the 75 percent of the normally colored babies are fully normal and which are heterozygous (see Punnett Square, Figure 3).*

	a	A
a	aa	aA
A	aA	AA

Figure 3.

These are the everyday genetics of simple dominant and recessive traits. But things aren't always that easy. Sometimes two different alleles result in young that look like both parents. Paul Hollander, a geneticist at Iowa State University, was kind enough to explain how this works. In a case like this, if a red flower is fertilized with a white flower, the first generation or the F1 generation is all pink. When you self-fertilize the pinks (breed them to each other), you get 25 percent red, 50 percent pink, and 25 percent white. If you self-fertilize the red plants, you get all red offspring; if you self-fertilize the whites, you get all white offspring. There are three phenotypes at work here: red, white, and pink. (The newer form of writing alleles is to use one letter with a superscript for the normal allele, so an albino would be a, the normal a+, red is WW, white is W+W+, and pink is WW+. This is called codominance, and as Paul Hollander says, you can easily tell which offspring are heterozygous.)

Codominance appears in some snake species. The hypomelanistic strain of the common boa is one example. This snake, when bred to the homozygous normal common boa, results in the heterozygous tiger, which is intermediate in appearance between the two. There are three genotypes and three phenotypes. (Be aware that terminology for this sort of phenomenon is not yet nailed down, and that you may also hear terms such as "incomplete dominant" or "partial dominant.") For boa breeding, the term codominance is well enough accepted to avoid confusion.

With the number of variants now available in many species, these examples are the mere tip of a very big genetic iceberg. Some boas may be heterozygous for two or more traits, and spontaneous color and pattern aberrations seem to turn up annually.

About Tyrosinase

There are certainly several genes that contribute to albinism, and the gene that controls tyrosinase production is one of them. Tyrosinase is produced in melanophores, the cells that produce black and brown pigments. Tyrosinase, a copper-containing enzyme, breaks apart tyrosine, an amino acid, to create melanin. No tyrosinase means no melanin, and hence no dark coloration. If an animal cannot produce tyrosinase, it is said to be tyrosinase-negative, a type of albinism.

But a tyrosinase-positive animal is also a type of albino. In this case the melanophore can produce tyrosinase, but it either cannot import the tyrosine or there's a blockage (as yet unknown) that prevents the tyrosinase from acting on the tyrosine. Both the tyrosinase-positive (T+) and the tyrosinase-negative (T−) types can also have other mutations that contribute to their degree and type of albinism.

You can often look at an albino reptile and make a good guess about the tyrosinanse + or −. The colors displayed tend to be muted, or less contrasting, in the t-negative specimens. When a t-negative specimen is bred to a t-positive specimen, the resulting offspring are *normally* colored, but are doubly heterozygous (heterozygous for both factors). This means that a percentage of albino babies will be produced whether the specimen is bred to a t-negative or a t-positive partner. If you want to be certain about the tyrosinase-positive or -negative quality of a reptile, you'll need to submit a fresh piece of the animal's skin to a lab for what's called a *dopa reaction.* The skin is incubated for a specified length of time in a solution of dopa. If tyrosinase is present (tyrosinase-positive), it reacts with the dopa and the melanophores turn dark due to the melanin they have produced.

Albinism: It was once thought that albinism involved a total lack of pigmentation and that albino organisms necessarily had pink irises and a dark red pupil. As now understood, albinism is simply a deficiency, but not necessarily a total lack, of pigmentation. The animal is of lighter (usually much lighter) than normal coloration, may be somewhat translucent (especially as a baby), and may have either blue or pink irises and dark red pupils. Reference is often made by herpetoculturists breeding corn snakes to red albinos and white albinos, the differentiation being the intensity of the red coloration displayed.

Amelanism: The condition known as amelanism (meaning literally "without black," a form of albinism) is characterized by a total lack of melanin. This is the term now used by hobbyists to describe red-eyed whitish reptiles of many species and lineages.

Anerythrism: Anerythrism is a term used by hobbyists to describe the lack of red pigment. Since a single type of color-containing cell, the xanthophore, is responsible for both red and yellow pigmentation, the phenomenon is the same as axanthism (literally "without yellow").

Hypomelanism: Hypomelanism is a variable and often naturally occurring reduction of dark pigment (hypo means "reduced"). Hypomelanistic boas are now integral in the breeding programs of many hobbyists.

Leucism: Although it is well documented in other species, leucism is virtually unknown in boas. Because in leucism all chromatophores of all colors are defective, leucistic herps are pure white, lacking pattern, but have dark (often blue) eyes. Occasionally, patches of dark coloration may appear with age, giving the animal a piebald appearance.

Melanism: Melanism is the term used to define an excess of dark pigmentation caused by the pigment melanin. Some boas, such as the Argentinian race, are strongly melanistic at birth, and become even more so with growth.

Pattern anomalies: Pattern anomalies (such as striping) are now as commonplace in captive-bred snakes as are aberrant colors. Striped boas are now readily available.

Caging

Suitable caging for a baby red-tailed boa or other boa constrictor is easily found and relatively inexpensive. Finding suitable caging for an adult is a little more problematic, but far from insurmountable.

A 15-inch-long (37-cm) baby boa can be housed in a tightly lidded 20-gallon (75.7-L) aquarium/terrarium; the floor space provided for one or two babies should be a minimum of 12 × 30 inches (30 × 76 cm). A very real advantage to these enclosures is their ready availability in virtually any size needed and the wonderful viewability they provide the keeper. The lids are also readily available at many pet stores and may incorporate screen (not your best choice) or strong ¼-inch (6-mm) wire mesh in sturdy plastic or metal frames. To avoid escape the lid must be firmly clipped or locked in place. Other style terraria, some with built-in sliding and lockable tops, are now available from many sources.

Some keepers house their baby and midsized boas in plastic sweater and blanket boxes with suitable floor dimensions. We feel that since boas evolved as climbers, the low containers are not as useful as a taller cage would be. Additionally, the lids do not latch as securely as we would like and their semiopaque walls render easy viewing of the snakes an impossibility. Adequate ventilation can be provided by drilling holes through the upper portions of the plastic sides. Use care when drilling, as the drill pressure can crack the more rigid forms of plastic unless you proceed slowly. These containers are certainly inexpensive, are available in many sizes, are easily cleaned, and when lidded can be stacked to save space.

Racks: Racks that hold a number of trays can be purchased or built. Usually they are designed so that the shelves of the rack are actually the top of the receptacle underneath, negating the need for the cumbersome and difficult-to-lock plastic tops.

As the boa grows, larger cages will of course be necessary. These can be built by you or purchased commercially. Budget now for this sort of expenditure.

For one or a pair of 6-footers (183 cm), a minimum floor space of 6 × 2.5 feet (183 × 74 cm) is suggested. Height should be at least 2 feet (61 cm), but if taller and properly outfitted with shelves or branches, the space will be utilized by the snakes.

Cage furniture: Cage furniture in the form of sizable limbs (at least 1½ times the diameter of your boa), a hide box, an easily cleaned water dish, and a substrate should be provided.

Be sure no furniture can shift or topple and injure your snake. As with the terrarium, the cage must be tightly closed and latchable or lockable. The substrate should be of absorbable or readily replaceable material. Newspaper, packing corrugate, paper towels, dry leaves (we use those of live oak), or dry mulch can be used.

Heat: Boas hide much of the time, but might come out on cool days to bask under a heat-providing lamp. Be sure that the snakes cannot come in contact with a bare bulb or ceramic heating unit, or they will burn themselves. Snakes in the wild don't come into contact with objects hot enough to burn them, and so have no "capability," if you'd like to call it, to connect the sensation of being burned with an object in their cage. Thermal burns are also possible from commercially available "hot rocks." We advise against the use of these.

There are other ways to heat a cage, in addition to a shield "hot spot" light or a ceramic bulb. Thermostatically controlled undercage heating pads may be used. What you need to provide is a cage temperature of 78 to 82°F (25–28°C) nights and 85 to 90°F (29–32°C) days (see comments on page 37 regarding cooler temperatures needed for cycling your boas for breeding). Heat only one end of the tank to provide a thermal gradient. A natural photoperiod, one allied with sunup and sundown, is best.

Bob Guerriere houses his breeder boas in spacious, temperature-controlled cages.

Drooping vines form an ideal resting place for this Bolivian boa.

Many Argentine boas are of dark coloration, lacking most traces of red or pink.

A one-third-grown rat makes little body distension in this 28-inch-long (70-cm) Bolivian boa.

colors, patterns, and the mystique that accompanies all giant snakes, is what makes boas so popular with both beginning and advanced hobbyists. However, stimulated by the smell of food, even very tame boas may bite at feeding time. Be sure to wash the scent of prey from your hands and arms, and approach the snakes carefully at that time.

The occasional boa that is a reluctant feeder will usually readily accept prey if it is offered in the evening when the snake is in the seclusion and security of its hide box. As a rule of thumb, the largest meal you feed your snake should not greatly exceed the diameter of your snake's head. The bigger boas do need slightly larger food, in the form of large rats, rabbits, or chickens.

Force-feeding

Occasionally a boa may refuse to begin eating voluntarily, no matter what ploys you try. In this case only, offer the snake a live rat pup or a live mouse. As a last resort, force-feeding may be necessary. To accomplish this, hold your boa gently but firmly behind its head. With blunt forceps, gently push the nose and shoulders of a freshly killed small mouse into the snake's mouth and partway into its throat. Then, making sure the snake doesn't dislodge the mouse, gently and slowly put the snake back on the floor of its cage, release your grip, and move your hands slowly away. After a time or two of this, the snake may decide to finish swallowing the mouse, and to eat voluntarily in the future.

In extreme cases, it may be necessary to force-feed the snake by using a syringelike pinky pump (available from reptile-specialist dealers) with a nozzlelike extension on the end. Thawed pinkies are placed in the body of the pump, a little water or appetite stimulant added, the nozzle is lubricated with vegetable oil, and the food is syringed down the throat of the boa. Do not obstruct the snake's glottis while force-feeding it by either method. Force-feeding can be very hard on a snake, especially if done by an inexperienced keeper. Use extreme care and ask the help of an experienced hobbyist if necessary. Often, the little snake will begin eating on its own after a time or two of syringing, but some don't and will ultimately die.

Health

Although you may give your boa the best possible husbandry, with a steady supply of fresh drinking water, an ample diet, and a sufficiently large and clean cage at the proper temperature, there are apt to be other health concerns as well.

Medical Issues

Most health problems are easily prevented. Most respond well to treatment, but a few are to be avoided because they are irreversible, extremely communicable, and eventually fatal.

External Parasites

Ticks and mites are external parasites that are rather easily combated. Ticks, usually present only on imported snakes but occasionally encountered if you maintain your boas outside during the summer months, are best removed manually. Ticks, in case you've never found one feeding on a pet dog (or worse, on yourself after a walk in the woods), are 8-legged parasites that look a bit like raisins but once they've fed on you, your dog, or your snake, feel soft, like a grape. Grasp the tick with forceps or a tick remover and pull gently while slowly rotating the forceps. The reason you rotate the tick puller or the forceps is

to ensure that the mouthparts can't clamp down and get left in your snake while you pull the body of the tick off. Be certain that the head parts are removed intact.

Mites are tiny arthropods that can multiply quickly into vast numbers if not combated. They have been implicated in the transmission of very serious, usually fatal diseases, such as inclusion body disease, known as IBD. If infested with mites, your snake will often rub its face and body along a shelf or perch, twitch, or soak incessantly in its water bowl. Do not overlook these pests.

There are several ways to deal with mites. Soaking your snake in tepid water for 20 minutes at a time was the time-honored (and largely ineffective) way to dispose of mites. There are a few products on the market designed specifically to deal with mites. You can buy these at your local pet store or order them on-line. You can use airborne insecticides such as "No-Pest," dust your snake with Sevin or DryDie (best in low-humidity situations), or spray the snake and its enclosure with dilute Ivermectin (available at your local feed store).

If you use a No-Pest strip, you'll need a piece only about 1 inch (2.5 cm) square. Remove the water container from the cage, and secure

The small, raised black dots on the anterior snout of this baby Bolivian boa are snake mites—tiny ectoparasites that are able to transmit diseases to snakes.

the piece of No-Pest near the top of the cage, where the snake cannot come into direct contact with it. You can put the piece on top of the cage, if the top is screen, or you can put it inside the snipped-off toe of a sock and secure the fabric near the top of the cage with tape or a thumbtack. Leave the piece in place for three days, then take it away and replace the cleaned and refilled water dish.

Since most treatments destroy only the mites themselves, leaving their eggs still viable, you'll need to

Ticks, as seen here, are easily eradicated ectoparasites.

repeat the treatment nine days later or you'll be back where you started.

Internal Parasites

Internal parasites (endoparasites) may occur in boids. Nematodes, cestodes, and/or protozoa may be present. Current thinking is that some may actually be beneficial to your snake and you may not need to worry about them, but your veterinarian is the one to ask. We suggest that you consult your veterinarian to determine if he or she thinks treatment is necessary.

Burns

The problem of thermal burns from a malfunctioning hot rock or improperly baffled bulb or ceramic heater is one that should never occur. Prevention is the best treatment. The primitive nervous system of a boa may allow these snakes to rest against a nonshielded light bulb or an overheating hot rock, all the while burning themselves severely. Carefully shield all exposed light bulbs or ceramic heating units with a wire net or cage, taking care that there are no sharp edges on which the snake can injure itself. Rather than hot rocks, use thermostatically controlled under-terrarium heaters to elevate cage temperature. Should a burn occur, it should be dressed with an antibacterial burn ointment. Seek veterinary assessment if serious.

Bites

Rodent bites can be very serious. Although it is true that snakes are predators that usually successfully overcome their prey with no incident, this is not always the case. Mice, rats, even rabbits and chickens, have been

A dark, red-suffused ground color is typical of boas from Corn Island.

Boas from Guyana often have a rich body color and maroon tail blotches.

This 5-foot-long (152-cm) Peruvian boa assumed an aggressive attitude when encountered on a night walk.

known to seriously injure the snakes in whose cages they have been left. Snakes will often shy away from an aggressive rodent. Once bitten by its intended prey, many snakes will not make any effort to kill the animal, no matter how hungry the snake may be. Even while being constricted, a rodent may injure your boa. Blindness may result from a bite to the eye. Mouth rot (infectious stomatitis) may develop from a bite or a scratch to the gums or mouth interior. Gaping wounds have been chewed into the sides of a snake by an unmonitored rat. A struggling rabbit may actually disembowel a snake with a single lucky kick. Baby chicks and chickens have injured boas' eyes by pecking at them. We urge that all prey animals be prekilled or, if for some reason they are not, that they are never left unwatched in your boa's cage. If your snake is bitten, dress the injury with antibacterial powder. If the bites are serious, immediately seek veterinary assessment.

Mouth Rot

Mouth rot can occur if a snake's teeth are broken, the mouth lining is injured, or if a struggling rodent being constricted bites the snake. The medication of choice may be Neosporin or a liquid sulfa drug. We have found both sulfamethazine and sulfathiazole sodium to be effective. If advanced to the stage where the snake's jawbones are affected and its teeth are loosened, veterinary assistance should be sought. This is a disfiguring disease that can be fatal if not treated.

Respiratory Infections

Respiratory ailments, typified by open-mouthed breathing, wheezing, or bubbling saliva, can occur if the temperature in your boa's cage is suboptimal, especially if humidity is high or the cage is damp. Not all causatives respond to the same antibiotic. Sensitivity tests must be made. Although, unlike many snakes, boas have two functional lungs, an untreated respiratory ailment can become quickly debilitating and, if unchecked, eventually fatal. Make certain that your cage temperatures are between 80 and 90°F (27–32°C), and seek veterinary assessment and help.

Blister Syndrome

Blister syndrome (the causative agents for this can be many) would be better called vesicular dermatitis. The snake's skin is spotted by small, pale, elongated spots that on close examination prove to be fluid-filled blisters. It is an insidious disease that is difficult to cure, and can be fatal. It can occur if the cage is too humid (especially, when the cage is very humid *and* suboptimally cool), when substrate remains too wet over a period of a day or more (especially if the cage is both wet and dirty), or if your snake soaks for excessively long periods in its water bowl. Again, prevention is the best avenue of defense. Be sure the water in your snake's bowl is clean and that the snake does not soak continuously for more than half a day. If your snake soaks excessively, take it out and examine it; often boas will soak in an effort to rid themselves of mites. Keep cage temperatures optimal. Prevent excessive humidity by providing adequate air flow and cage ventilation. Keep substrate dry and clean.

Should vesicular dermatitis occur, immediately assess and correct your

Although referred to as the Madagascar tree boa, this beautiful and variably colored snake actually spends much time on the ground.

Some Mexican boas, like this example from the state of Colima, are of very dark color.

regimen of husbandry and seek the help of a reptile-oriented veterinarian. If the serum-containing blisters are many or if skin damage is apparent, lesions may already be present on internal organs. Sensitivity tests are necessary, and antibiotic treatment will necessarily be lengthy.

Inclusion Body Disease

Inclusion body disease (IBD) is a very communicable, insidious, and eventually fatal viral affliction of boas and pythons. It has no known cure. If your boa is afflicted with this readily spread disease, it will develop a regurgitation syndrome, mouth rot, bloating, and a lack of body coordination. "Stargazing," when the head and neck are held up or contorted, is also a symptom. This disease is especially prevalent in red-tailed boas. It is highly contagious to other boid snakes in the collection. Isolate and quarantine any snake acting suspiciously, then immediately consult your veterinarian.

Popeye

In popeye, the space between the eye and the brill (eyecap) becomes filled with discolored serum. This may be due to infection of the eye, infection or injury to the related ducts, or other causes. Blindness or loss of the eye may result. Consult a veterinarian promptly.

Shedding

It is important that your snake shed fully at the proper time. A failed shed can lead to serious health issues. Improper shedding (retained eyecaps,

and so on) may occasionally occur if your boa is not properly hydrated or if the cage humidity is too low. A drop of mineral oil on the remaining area of skin will usually soften it and allow careful removal. If the eyecaps are not shed after softening with mineral oil, carefully grasp the flange of old skin usually left in the orbit and lift gently upward. Bits of skin may adhere to the tail tip impeding circulation and eventually causing the loss of the tail tip. Remove this promptly. Always remove skin from the snake's head by pulling retained skin in the direction of the tail.

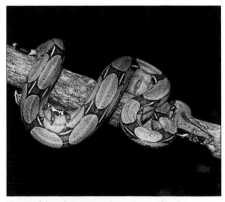

Boas, like this Peruvian one, climb readily and with agility.

Breeding

With the availability of color and pattern morphs, such as albino, snow, Arabesque, striped, salmon, and super salmon, it may seem that all of these were effortless accomplishments. In truth, these successes were a very long time in coming.

Imported boas, even well-acclimated, very long-term captive imported boas, were once considered notoriously difficult to breed. Many breeders tried breeding these snakes, but relatively few succeeded, and even fewer succeeded in breeding boas with any regularity. The "problems" surrounding the captive production of these snakes took on almost mythic proportions.

Finally, though, as hobbyists learned more about the stimuli needed to cycle boas reproductively, breeding successes became more common, and as is the case with many snakes, the F2s—the second generation of captive-born boas—proved more amenable to captive breeding programs than the originals.

We have found, as with other more readily bred giant snakes, the reproductive cycle of a boa is triggered by a combination of the snake's good health, a genetically compatible, receptive partner, and naturally occurring atmospheric and climatic phenomena, such as photoperiod, relative humidity, barometric pressure, and rainfall.

These stimuli are as important to captive snakes as they are to those in the wild and it is by duplicating as many of them as possible that you will most reliably cycle your red-tailed boa and common boa reproductively.

Feeding

Because a boa's digestive ability is compromised when its metabolism slows, it is necessary that you stop feeding your boas about two weeks prior to the beginning of its winter's cooling; however, fresh water should always be available. This hiatus of a fortnight between the last meal and the period of cooling will allow the full digestion and the completion of related bodily functions. If your boa is of an equatorial form that will only have its cage temperature reduced slightly, you may continue feeding the snakes, but reduce the relative size of the meal and the frequency with which feeding occurs. A good rule of thumb is to allow your cooled boa to digest its meal fully and to stool before feeding it again. If your boa is to undergo a more radical cage temperature reduction, it should not be fed at all from two weeks before the cooling until the cage temperature is elevated again.

When startled, many boas (such as this Corn Island boa) hide their head within body coils.

Cage Temperature

A cage temperature reduction to 69 to 72°F (20–22°C) at night and 79 to 84°F (26–29°C) during the hours of daylight will usually successfully cycle equatorial boas. Although this daytime temperature is suitable for boas such as races from Argentina and the common boas from the northern half of that subspecies' range, for these, nighttime cage temperatures should range between 60 to 64°F (15.5–18°C)

What effect do photoperiod, temperature, and relative humidity have on the reproductive cycling of boas?

Many snakes, even equatorial snakes, become seasonally quiescent, or at least less active, during the winter months. It is then when, except at the equator, photoperiods are shortest, and temperatures and humidity are the lowest (yes, this is true even at the equator!). It is during this time of comparative rest that both the female and male boa constrictors begin their reproductive cycle. Follicular development (females) and gonad recrudescence (males) begins. Reptile physiologists believe that the inevitable parade of the seasons stimulates these reproductive system changes, and readies the snakes for successful breeding when their period of activity resumes. Plain and simple, fewer hours of daylight and/or even marginally cooler temperatures, lower humidity, and reduced rainfall stimulate wild boas to breed.

By providing your sexually mature captive boas with fewer hours of illumination, nighttime cooling, and lower cage humidity, you are sim-ulating the conditions they undergo in the wild. Lowering humidity is most easily done by increasing ventilation within the cage, especially when home heating units, which dramatically lower available humidity, are in use, or by removing the water bowl during the day. After six to eight weeks, increase the photoperiod, temperature, and relative humidity in your boa's cage. This can be done gradually or immediately, as you prefer. After the boa is again active and cage parameters are back to normal, feed your boas. Once the temperatures are at their normal high, periodically mist the cage and the snakes.

Despite our ever-increasing knowledge, the breeding of boas remains just a little "iffy." Some examples breed readily; others do not. Captive-born boas often breed more readily than wild-collected ones. It may take wild-collected boas many years to acclimate sufficiently to breed in captivity, but then, if you start out with immature captive-born boas, it will take them several years to attain sexual maturity. Even the rather insignificant action of moving proven breeders to a new cage or, more especially, moving or shipping them to a new home, has been known to curtail breeding activities by the snakes for one year or more while they again settle in. Boas seem to know instinctively how to keep us humble! And of the boas, it is rather generally conceded by herpetoculturists that the eagerly sought red-tail is the most difficult to successfully breed.

Additional Breeding Essentials

Let's further define and explore the various preparatory criteria:

Boa constrictors are viviparous (meaning they give birth to living young). It is likely that if she becomes gravid, the female will bask extensively, and may even lie partially on her side (do not mistake this behavior for the onset of inclusion body disease [see page 35]) to better facilitate elevating her body temperature. After a gestation of 170 to 250 days—temperature and other factors dictate gestation

duration—a female may have as few as 10 or as many as 50 babies. Infertile egg masses and some dead babies are often produced with the clutch. Some babies eat before their first (postnatal) shed, but may fast until after shedding. Females often eat the infertile egg masses, and may occasionally cannibalize the live neonates. During and following parturition a female may also lie on top of a newborn, killing it. Hide

The approaching camera has this Bolivian boa seeking scent cues.

This is a young adult Hog Island boa.

Note the catlike elliptical pupil of this Bolivian boa.

This boa from Suriname lacks typical lateral markings.

boxes into which the babies may escape should be provided.

A sexually mature female red-tailed boa may ovulate and form infertile egg masses even without the presence of a male. The same expenditure of energy may occur if a female breeds with a genetically incompatible male. What makes two snakes genetically incompatible is entirely conjectural. Sometimes boas that seem to be nearly identical in every respect fail to breed successfully; in other cases boas that are obviously divergent—even of different races and that are obviously from very different origins—breed successfully. Purchasing already proven pairs (pairs that have bred and successfully produced young) is possible, but often quite expensive.

Health

Because breeding can be physically demanding on boas, it is absolutely necessary that your potential breeders be in the best health. Male red-tails that are reproductively active may refuse food for a few days or even several weeks. Since the breeding season closely follows emergence from a period of winter inactivity during which food has been withheld or reduced in quantity, the time lapse between meals can easily be a third of the year. During this period of fasting, energy reserves are continually being drawn upon. Because of this it is mandatory that your boa's weight and health are optimum when the cooling period begins.

At a Glance: Reproductive Cycling of Your Boa

Although the boas of tropical regions do not undergo an actual seasonal dormancy, during the coolest, shortest, and driest days of winter, even those from equatorial regions may become quiescent. During this period of relative inactivity the feeding urge is usually lessened considerably. The breeding of red-tailed boas in the wild is triggered by normal climatic warming following the several weeks, or months, of winter.

It is by duplicating as many of these conditions as possible that you will most reliably cycle your boa reproductively.

In sequence of importance, the steps would be

Cooling
- Have a pair of sexually mature boas from the same geographic region; some breeders advocate keeping the sexes separated during the cooling period.
- Your boas must be healthy and have "good" body weight.
- Stop feeding your boas about two weeks prior to the beginning of their cooling. Fresh water must always be available though.
- During your winter months, cool your boas for a period of six to twelve weeks (many breeders suggest eight weeks) to 68 to 72°F (18.5–21.5°C) nights and 79 to 84°F (26–29°C) days.

Genetic Incompatibility

Maybe genetic incompatibility is at fault. Genetic incompatibility is a catchall term, meaning it's used when no other explanation seems to fit. It generally means that snakes from different areas do not conceive. It can be especially difficult to ascertain with imported boas. One of the surest ways—but not a guaranteed way—to avoid this diagnosis is to buy the pair at the same time, from the same dealer, and from the same imported group of snakes. This will probably ensure that your boas are from the same general region.

Genetic compatibility is important not only to assure that your boas can breed successfully and that the developing young are viable, but also to assure that unnecessary stress is not put on the breeders.

"Slugs": A breeding male may be off feed for weeks, and when gravid the female may cease to feed as well. Whether the developing egg masses are fertile or not (infertile egg masses are often referred to as "slugs"), the same energy reserves that would have been used if the breeding had been successful are being drawn upon. If either of your breeding boas begins

- Reduce photoperiod; this is most important for boas originating from several degrees or farther south or north of the equator.
- Reduce cage humidity.

Warming

Little preparation need be made to rewarm your boas. They may be warmed and have cage humidity elevated simultaneously. Increase and maintain a natural photoperiod. After a few days of being warmed, the snakes may be fed. If you have been maintaining them separately, now is the time to put them together. If the snakes are compatible, breeding may begin almost immediately, or it might not begin until the female has had a post-hibernation skin shed. It is at that time that the female's stimulatory pheromone (reproductive stimulatory scents) production seems strongest, and breeding is most apt to occur. Breeding may be stimulated by adding a second male (see the cautionary note on page 42) or by misting the cage and the snakes. The snakes may mate several times during the season. Once breeding has begun, some males may fast anywhere from one or two to five or six weeks. Gravid females also fast for several weeks. It is for this reason that it is so important that the snakes be healthy and heavy at the onset of the cycling sequence.

This 8-foot-long (244-cm) boa was found in a village near Iquitos, Peru.

the breeding sequence at suboptimal body weight, it may become seriously debilitated by the time the breeding season draws to a close. Separating the snakes early does not mean that they will resume feeding even one day sooner than Mother Nature intended.

Sexual Maturity

Boa constrictors are medium-sized to large snakes that normally take several years to mature. Like most other reptiles, sexual maturity is dictated by both size *and* age, and growth rate is dependent on food intake. A red-tailed boa can have its growth "pushed" if it is fed much and often. The size normally attained in three or four years can be reached in two years. Besides early adulthood, early sexual maturity will also be attained by the snake. But is this early attaining of adulthood in the best interest of the snake? Probably not, for it has been shown time and again that a snake so pushed will not only produce a relatively small first clutch with a higher than normal percentage of infertility and neonate abnormalities, but that this problem may manifest itself for several additional clutches. It would seem far better to allow the snake to

A portrait of a juvenile Hog Island boa.

Boas, such as this juvenile, are often encountered on the ecotours we lead in Peru.

take the normally needed additional year or two to attain breeding size. Does normal (slow) growth assure a greater percentage of viable babies when the boa is bred? It does seem to increase the odds that the babies *will* be normal and healthy.

Separating the Sexes

In the belief (perhaps rightly so) that absence makes the heart grow fonder, some boa breeders advocate keeping the sexes separated for varying periods. Some successful breeders of red-tailed boas keep the two sexes together only during the breeding period. Other equally successful breeders suggest a cooling period for varying periods. (Yet others, us included, have not found the separation of the sexes a necessity.) Sexual activity by your boas can be stimulated by introducing a second adult male boa from another colony to the breeding cage. The two males will usually begin ritualized combat. (If overt aggression occurs, remove the second male immediately; take care to avoid being bitten during the removal.) The combat will progress to the newly stimulated dominant male breeding the female.

Gravid Females

Provide bred females with warmth and a large hiding area. A basking area with an air temperature of from 88 to 92°F (31–33°C) and a substrate temperature (at the hot spot) of from 94 to 105°F (34–40.5°C) will usually be used extensively by gestating female boas of all subspecies; remember not to heat the entire cage to this range, but only a limited part of the cage. Improper temperatures will often result in aborted undeveloped egg masses or partially developed or deformed young. Even a short period of improper temperature may result in aberrant patterns or other (usually unwanted) abnormalities. The fact that many of the female boas imported while gravid either abort or give birth to deformed babies strongly suggests that gravid females should be disturbed as little as possible or not actually handled at all.

Glossary

Albino: Lacking black pigment.

Ambient temperature: The temperature of the surrounding environment.

Anal plate: The large scute immediately anterior to the cloaca.

Anerythristic: Lacking red pigment.

Anterior: Toward the front.

Anus: The external opening of the cloaca; the vent.

Boid/Boidae: The grouping of snakes containing the boas and pythons.

Brille: The transparent "spectacle" covering the eyes of a snake.

Brumation: Term often used to describe reptilian and amphibian hibernation.

Caudal: Pertaining to the tail.

cb/cb: Captive bred, captive born.

Cloaca: The common chamber into which digestive, urinary, and reproductive systems empty and that itself opens exteriorly through the vent or anus.

Cloacal spur: A movable spur on each side of the vent.

Constricting: To wrap tightly in coils and squeeze; death is due to suffocation.

Crepuscular: Active at dusk and/or dawn.

Deposition site: The spot chosen by the female to lay her eggs or have young.

Dimorphic: A difference in form, build, or coloration involving the same species; often sex-linked.

Diurnal: Active in the daytime.

Dorsal: Pertaining to the back; upper surface.

Dorsolateral: Pertaining to the upper sides.

Dorsum: The upper surface.

Ecological niche: The precise habitat utilized by a species.

Ectothermic: "Cold-blooded."

Endothermic: "Warm-blooded."

Erythristic: A prevalence of red pigment.

Form: An identifiable species or subspecies.

Genotype: The explanation of both dominant and recessive genes present.

Genus: A taxonomic classification of a group of species having similar characteristics. The genus falls between the next higher designation of "family" and the next lower designation of "species." *Genera* is the plural of genus. It is always capitalized when written.

Glottis: The opening of the windpipe.

Gravid: The reptilian equivalent of mammalian pregnancy.

Heliothermic: Describing an animal that basks in the sun to thermoregulate.

Hemipenes: The dual copulatory organs of male lizards and snakes.

Hemipenis: The singular form of hemipenes.

Herpetoculture: The captive breeding of reptiles and amphibians.

Herpetoculturist: One who indulges in herpetoculture.

Herpetologist: One who indulges in herpetology.

Herpetology: The study (often scientifically oriented) of reptiles and amphibians.

Hydrate: To restore body moisture by drinking or absorption.

Hypomelanistic: Showing an inordinate amount of red pigment.

Insular: As used here, island-dwelling.

Intergrade: Offspring resulting from the breeding of two contiguous subspecies.

Jacobson's organs: Highly enervated olfactory pits in the palate of snakes and lizards.

Juvenile: A young or immature specimen.

Labial: Pertaining to the lips.

Labial pit(s): Heat sensory depressions on the lips of some boas.

Lateral: Pertaining to the side.

Melanism: A profusion of black pigment.

Mental: The scale at the tip of the lower lip.

Middorsal: Pertaining to the middle of the back.

Midventral: Pertaining to the center of the belly or abdomen.

Monotypic: A taxonomic group containing only one representative of a subordinate group, such as a genus with only one species.

Morph: A color or pattern variant for a specific species.

Nocturnal: Active at night.

Ocular stripe: A stripe on the side of the head that passes through the eye.

Ontogenetic: Age-related (color) changes.

Ovoviviparous: Bearing live young.

Phenotype: The expression of the genes, as in the animal's appearance.

Photoperiod: The daily/seasonally variable length of the hours of daylight.

Poikilothermic: A species with no internal body temperature regulation. The old term was "cold-blooded."

Postocular: To the rear of the eye.

Race: A subspecies.

Rostral: The (often modified) scale on the tip of the snout.

Scute: A large scale.

Species: A group of similar creatures that produce viable young when breeding. The taxonomic designation that falls beneath genus and above subspecies. Abbreviation: "sp."

Spurs: The external remnant of hind limbs, one on each side of a boa's cloaca.

Subcaudal: Beneath the tail.

Subspecies: The subdivision of a species. A race that may differ slightly in color, size, scalation, or other criteria. Abbreviation: "ssp."

Sympatric: Occurring together.

Taxonomy: The science of classification of plants and animals.

Terrestrial: Land-dwelling.

Thermoregulate: To regulate (body) temperature by choosing a warmer or cooler environment.

Vent: The external opening of the cloaca; the anus.

Venter: The underside of a creature; the belly.

Ventral: Pertaining to the undersurface or belly.

Ventrolateral: Pertaining to the sides of the venter (belly).

Special Interest Groups

Herpetological Societies

Reptile and amphibian hobbyists and professionals interact via clubs, monthly magazines, professional societies, and at herp expos.

Herpetological societies (or clubs) are found in North America, Europe, and other areas of the world. Most have monthly meetings, some publish newsletters, many host or sponsor field trips, picnics, or seminars and symposiums. Among the members are enthusiasts of varying expertise. Information about these clubs can often be learned by querying pet shop employees, science teachers, university biology department professors, or curators or employees at the department of herpetology at local museums and zoos. All such clubs welcome inquiries and new members.

Two of the professional herpetological societies are

Society for the Study of Amphibians and Reptiles (SSAR)
Department of Zoology
Miami University
Oxford, OH 45056

Herpetologists' League
c/o Texas National Heritage Program
Texas Parks and Wildlife Department
4200 Smith School Road
Austin, TX 78744

The SSAR publishes two quarterly journals: *Herpetological Review* contains husbandry, range extensions, news on ongoing field studies, and so on, while the *Journal of Herpetology* contains articles more oriented toward academic herpetology.

Reptiles Magazine publishes articles on all aspects of herpetology and herpetoculture (including boa constrictors). This monthly also carries classified ads and news about herp expos.

Reptiles Magazine
P.O. Box 6050
Mission Viejo, CA 92690

One of the most important Internet addresses is *www.kingsnake.com*. This site provides an immensely active classified section, interactive forums, periodic chats, and web radio interviews. Because of the ability to post and view photos of the boas being offered for sale, this site should be of great interest to all hobbyists.

Index

Page numbers set in boldface type indicate photographs.